QUEEN ELIZABETH'S DEFENCE
OF HER PROCEEDINGS
IN CHURCH AND STATE

WITH AN INTRODUCTORY ESSAY ON
THE NORTHERN IRELAND REBELLION

BY

WILLIAM EDWARD COLLINS

PUBLISHED FOR THE CHURCH HISTORICAL SOCIETY

LONDON
S · P · C · K
1958

*First published in 1899
(as No. LVIII of the Church
Historical Society Publications)
Reprinted in 1958*

*S.P.C.K.
Holy Trinity Church
Marylebone Road
London, N.W.1*

Printed in Great Britain by
THE SIDNEY PRESS LTD., LONDON AND BEDFORD
A Member of the Hazell-Sun Group

PREFATORY NOTE

THE desirability of reprinting Elizabeth's *Declaration* was originally suggested to me by the use which is made of it in the Bishop of London's noble biography of that Queen. Further examination showed that the copy in the Record Office contained corrections and additions in Elizabeth's own handwriting which had never been printed before; and this text was accordingly adopted.

The essay on the Northern Rebellion is the result of a study made for a special purpose, and is now prefixed to the *Declaration* as supplying some guide to the circumstances under which it was written.

W. E. COLLINS

Allhallows Barking, E.C.

CONTENTS

PREFATORY NOTE iv

THE NORTHERN REBELLION OF 1569 5

 I. Its Antecedents 7

 II. Its Course and Suppression 10

 III. Its Distinctively Religious Character 18

 IV. Provision for the Future 27

A DECLARATION OF THE QUEEN'S PROCEEDINGS SINCE
 HER REIGN 37

APPENDIX I. Letter of Pius V to the Rebel Earls 52

 II. Elizabeth's Declaration in the Star
  Chamber 60

THE NORTHERN REBELLION

THE importance of the Northern Rebellion of 1569 lies in the fact that it was a last trial of strength between the old religious order and the new; between the adherents of the Papacy and the English Church as reformed. To all appearance, the party of reaction had much to hope for from the contest. Queen Elizabeth's government during the last twelve years had given rise to much seething discontent, and it yet remained to be seen how strong and buoyant was the English life which it had fostered. The great lords were jealous and alarmed at the growing up of a new order of national life in which they were slowly but surely being elbowed from the foremost place. The uncertainty of the succession to the Crown dissatisfied the nation as a whole, which had already been called upon to suffer many things from the like uncertainty. The fact that Mary Queen of Scots was a prisoner in England aroused the ire of many, both at home and abroad: and the self-seeking and frivolity of some of Elizabeth's courtiers added largely to the general discontent. All these things might seem to give the leaders of a revolt every hope of success. So much of self-interest joined to so much of religious zeal could hardly be in vain.

The event proved otherwise. When the time came the recusants in most parts of the country held aloof, although they were doubtless ready to join in had there been any real hope of success. Even the politically dis-

appointed did not openly join hands with the rebels; and the forces of personal loyalty to Elizabeth proved to be far stronger than could have been expected. The appeal to arms revealed the fact that a continuous steady growth had been going on in spite of all the outward disorder; and the forces of reaction proved to be hopelessly outmatched. It would have been less remarkable had the struggle been more severe; and the real significance of the rebellion lies in the fact that it was such an utter fiasco. From henceforth there was little to be feared from popery[1]; and the really dangerous foe to the reformed English Church was recognized to be militant puritanism.

[1] There is a real difference in kind between this rebellion and the contemptible through dangerous plots and treasons which followed upon the publication of the Bull *Regnans in excelsis*.

I

THE religious antecedents of the revolt must be traced in somewhat greater detail.

It was only by slow degrees that order was developed out of the state of chaos in which English religion had been left at the death of Queen Mary. For although the great majority of Englishmen had accepted the Elizabethan settlement of religion without hesitation and often with enthusiasm, the disaffected minority was far from inconsiderable. Moreover, the settlement was itself as yet incomplete, and had still to acquire its stable character through actual working, under the wise guidance of Archbishop Parker and the yet wiser non-intervention of Elizabeth. The apparently unformed and tentative character of its system both gave a sense of insecurity to the loyal churchman, and caused the recusant to live in hope that the tide might once more turn in his favour.

Meanwhile Elizabeth's religious policy, judged by the standard of the day, was one of large-hearted toleration. The provisions of the Act of Uniformity against recusancy were allowed to remain inoperative to a considerable extent; and even the Oath of Supremacy was only very sparingly tendered. So long as her subjects were loyal and peaceable, the Queen was not concerned to trouble tender consciences needlessly. But this toleration, although it was winning over many who were originally disaffected, gave abundant opportunities for scheming on the part of those who were irrecon-

7

cilable. And as time went on, an ever-increasing number of secret emissaries of the Papacy found their way back into England from the Continent. They went from place to place, ostensibly to minister to their recusant brethren, but really stirring up disaffection on all hands, and endeavouring to withdraw those who were still doubtful from their loyalty to the English Church; sometimes, it would appear, even from their allegiance to the English Queen. And thus everything pointed to a new religious revolt before long: under such circumstances, in fact, it was inevitable.

But the immediate incentive to the rebellion came from events which were mainly political. In May 1568 Mary Queen of Scots had fled to England and thrown herself on the protection of Elizabeth, between whom and herself there was an old-standing rivalry. Since then she had been kept a close prisoner in the North, and had at once supplied a focus and an object for the smouldering disaffection. The communications between her adherents in England and the ambassador of Spain at once assumed a character which was dangerous to Elizabeth,[1] and the intrigues of the papal envoys began to take a bolder tone.[2] More than this, Mary's remarkable powers of fascination, under which

[1] See, for example, the letters of Don Guerau de Spes to Philip of Spain, dated 22 September, 8 October and 8 November 1569 (*Calendar of State Papers, Spanish*, Elizabeth, vol. ii, pp. 195, 198, 207). As late as 16 December Philip wrote to the Duke of Alva telling him that it lay with him to decide what was to be done, and adding, "We think here that the best course will be to encourage with money and secret favour the Catholics of the North, and to help those in Ireland to take up arms against the heretics and deliver the crown to the Queen of Scotland, to whom it belongs by succession. This course, it is presumed, would be very agreeable to the Pope and all Christendom, and would encounter no opposition from anyone" (ibid., ii, 217).

[2] See post, p. 12 f.

many of the English lords had already passed, now made themselves increasingly felt; and Elizabeth soon found that some of the chief noblemen of her realm, conformists as well as recusants, had come under the spell. A plan had been formed for the marriage of Mary with the Duke of Norfolk, the first subject of the realm, who had conscientiously conformed to the New Order, and never withdrew himself. Elizabeth was aware of it, and tried hard to give his aims a loyal direction. But it was in vain. Although the project did not in itself involve any unfaithfulness to his allegiance, his timidity and secrecy more than suggested that he was at heart disloyal. Meantime, intrigues of all kinds went on openly; whispers of revolt were in the air; Elizabeth was fairly alarmed. On 8 October 1569 a commission was issued for the arrest of the Duke, and he was lodged in the Tower. This step, if taken at an earlier time, might have stayed the movement; but preparations in the North had already gone too far, and an outbreak was now inevitable.

II

THE northern counties, far more sparsely populated and less advanced in the arts of civilization than the South, had also been more slowly affected by the reformation changes. The lawlessness of the border-lands provided constant work for the Wardens of the Marches; and the state of the Bishopric of Durham, and of Yorkshire and Lancashire, was not much better. The people were, in general, more attached to the ancient houses, the Dacres and Nevilles and Percies, than to those in authority; and the hearts of many of them yearned after the old services still. A letter written by Bishop Best of Carlisle to Cecil in 1561, whilst it shows that there was a general conformity, shows also how widespread this feeling was:

... Because yor hono^r maye better vnderstande ye state of thynges here by my doynges sithe my comynge hither, I will brevlie relate them vnto you. firste after three Smones made in the Cathedrall Churche (vnto wiche a gret nombre of all p̄tes adiacent did resorte) the comen people w^t moche reioyce affirmed they had bēn deceavid. Wiche also happened throughout all my visita-cōn in the diocesse ye two next weekes folowing. the gen-tilmen of the contrey receaved me in ev̄y place w^t moche Civilites. ... The preistes are wicked ympes of Anti-christ & for ye moste p̄te very ignorante & stubburne, past measure false and sotle. onlie feare maketh them obedient. onlie three absented themselues in my visita-cōn & fled because they wolde not subscribe. of ye w^e two belonge to my lord dacres & one to ye Earle of Cum-

berland, vnto wᵉ I have assigned dayes undre danger of
depᵛation. Aboute xij or xiij churches in gylsland all
vndre my lord Dacres do not appeare, but bearyng themselves upon my lorde refuse to come In. & at Stapilton
& sondrye of yᵉ other have yet masse openly. at whome
my lorde & his officers wynke. & although they stande
excommycate I do no furdre medle wᵗ them untill I have
some aide frome my lord psident & yᵉ coūsaile in yᵉ
northe lest I myghte trouble yᵉ contrey withe those yᵗ
in maner are desperate. & yet I doubte not but by polly-
cie to make them obedient at my lord Dacres comyng
into yᵉ Contrey. But I well pceave he is something so
myghtie in this contrey & as it were a prynce. & yᵉ lorde
warden of yᵉ weste marches of Scotland & he are but
to great frendes. It is judged of them yᵗ are wise yᵗ he
suffreth yᵉ Scottes to do harme in England vnponyshed
of pollicye, yᵉ rather to drawe home his frend my lord
Dacres, wᵉ is to longe (as his frendes here thynke) de-
teaned at london.[1] ...

Thus even as early as 1561 there could hardly have
been fitter soil for an outbreak than the North; and
eight years afterwards, although plans were being
formed in divers parts of the country, they of the North
were more eager than any, and far better prepared. So
when the vacillation and subsequent arrest of the Duke
of Norfolk dashed the hopes of others, and put an end
to their lukewarm zeal, it had no such result upon the
Northern gentlemen. Their plans were thrown into
confusion, they were divided in counsel, but they had
gone too far to be able to recede. The Earl of Northumberland's servant was sent to the Spanish ambassador,
Don Guerau de Spes, to say that they would release the
Queen of Scots, and take possession of the North, if the

[1] *S. P. Dom.* Eliz., xviii, 21; 21 July 1561.

King of Spain would but give them the help of a small number of harquebussiers.[2]

Again, whereas elsewhere the motive was largely mere discontent, a desire for the liberation of the Queen of Scots, the declaration of the succession, and the removal of Elizabeth's "evil counsellors", here the religious motive was really the moving principle. This was partly owing to the fact that, as has been said already, the reformation movement had not yet penetrated so deeply in the North, but still more owing to the scheming of papal agents from abroad.

That the Northern Rebellion was largely instigated by papal agency there can be no real doubt. English opinion was quite clear upon the point; and it is well summed up in Bishop Jewel's statement: "The coals were kindled here; but the bellows which gave the wind lay at Rome, and there sat he which made the fire."[3] We have express testimony to the fact in a letter of Pope Pius V directed to the rebel Earls[4]; and signs of the work of papal agents in England are of very frequent occurrence. The chief amongst these agents was one Dr Morton. Sanders expressly tells us that he had

[2] *Calendar of State Papers, Spanish*, Eliz., vol. ii, no. 199. Guerau de Spes to the King, 8 October: "The friends of the prisoners, who are the Earls of Northumberland, Westmorland, Cumberland, Derby, and many others, all Catholics, are much grieved at this cowardice, if such it can be called, of the Duke of Norfolk, and they have sent Northumberland's servant, who spoke to me before on the matter, to say that they will by armed force release the Queen [i.e., of Scots] and take possession of all the north country and effecting a general restitution of the goods of your Majesty's subjects within a year. They only ask that, after they have released the Queen, they should be aided by your Majesty with a small number of harquebussiers."

[3] Jewel, *A View of a Seditious Bull: Works*, Parker Society, iv, 1146. Cf. the Homily on Rebellion, the sixth part (ed. Corrie, p. 596).

[4] This letter is printed in the Appendix, No. I.

been sent into England by the Pope to denounce **Eliza-beth** as a heretic and *ipso facto* deposed.[5] The Bishop of Ross afterwards confessed that a large sum of money had been sent by the Pope through Morton to the rebels[6]; and this explains the fact that the Earls, notoriously poor men, were able to offer " 16[d] a day wages to all that will come."[7] Signs of Morton's secret work appear again and again; and when at length the question was mooted of publicly taking up arms against Elizabeth as a usurper, his name was brought forward as in favour of this course.[8]

[5] Sanders, *De Visib. Monarch.*, Lovanii 1571, p. 706; See also Tierney's Dodd, iii, 12 note; and Strype, *Annals* 11, i, 577. Laderchius says that the Pope sent Morton into England, and gives a letter from the Pope to Alva, dated 13 February 1569, in which he says: "Petimus a te, ut ejus desideria cognoscas, quae sunt illa quidem sancta, et pia, sed tamen talia ut Divinis potius quam humanis auxiliis indigere videantur"; and adds, "nobis visum est, neque virum hunc bonum ab instituto suo deterrere, neque te inscio, et absque consilio tuo aliquid esse tentandum" (Laderchii *Annales Ecclesiastici*, ii, 313 f., ed. Roma, 1733). Laderchi expressly derives the revolt from the fact that "summi Pastoris hi vocem audierunt".

[6] In his examination in the Tower, 29 November 1571, he deposed that the Pope sent twelve thousand crowns to the rebels in response to their letters "by the means of a Doctor called Morton, or some suchelyke name"; and that "he [the Bishop] was advertyced of the Distribucyon of the Twelve Thowsand Crownes amongst Thenglisshe Rebells by a letter sent unto hym from the Countesse of Northumberland" (Hatfield MS., 1734, printed in W. Murdin, *State Papers*, London, 1759, p. 60, i.e. *Burghley Papers*, vol. II).

[7] Sir John Foster to Sussex, 25 November: *S. P. Dom.* Eliz. Add. xv, 51[1].

[8] It is convenient to collect together some of the evidence upon this point. (*a*) Francis Norton, one of the sons of old Richard Norton, wrote to Leicester and Burghley from Antwerp on 2 April 1572: "It is very well known in the country that the said earl [Northumberland] and I were not friends, and dwelling both in our parishes, during the space of iii years, I never came in his house, nor company otherwise than by chance, whereas I never tarried, until such time as doctor Morton came into England from Rome, who used such persuasions to the said earl and to my father whom he had served in

times passed, and to many others where he had travelled to and fro in England for the said purpose, was the most earnest mover of the rebellion, showing as many reasons to make for his purpose, which we, by experience, find to be most untrue. . . . His first persuasion was to give us to understand of the excommunication which threatened to us (as he said) danger sundry ways, as well as touching our souls, as the loss of our country; giving us further to understand that all Christian princes, through the Pope's persuasions, would seek to subvert us, if we did not reform it within ourselves; affirming that he had travelled through the most parts of England, and did find the most part of the common people most inclined thereunto; if so be that any would once begin to take the enterprise in hand" (*S. P. Dom.*, Eliz., Add. xxi, 29; *Memorials of the Rebellion*, p. 280). (*b*) The Earl of Northumberland, in his answers to interrogatories, said: "There was a scruple and division amongst us, after the duke's first committing to the Tower, whether we ought by God's laws to rise against our Prince or no, being our anointed Prince. We referred the judgement thereof to learned men, and the same being demanded of a couple, the one being singularly well learned (whose name I know not) the other being Master Copley that reconciled me. Their judgements was (and showed us the scriptures) we ought not to wager battle against our anointed Princes unless they were lawfully excommunicated by the head of the Church. Then said the other party, that was thought to be a lawful excommunication when that the Pope did send unto the Queen's Majesty for sufferance to send his ambassadors unto her presence, which being denied, they said that doctor Morton's opinion was, for that cause her highness was lawfully excommunicated, and so consequently lawful to take arms against her. Thus much did Markenfeld report of the said Dr Morton being at that time beyond the seas. The most of us thought it was rather his own imagination to advance the matter than otherwise. Yet notwithstanding the other two divines thought it not sufficient unless the excommunication had been orderly published within the realm. This scruple did not only persuade Sir John Neville and me to forbear the matter but also occasioned sundry other gentlemen to withdraw themselves from us." *S. P. Dom.*, Eliz., Add. xxi, 56[1]. (*c*) William Lord Eure, writing to Cecil, reports the statement of Mr Smith of Eshe, one of the rebels, to Mr Tong: " 'Since the apprehension of the Duke of Norfolk the setting up of religion (meaning papistry) is our purpose.' Said Tong, 'How can that be but you shall be rebels to our quene and so do against your consciences.' 'No,' said Smith, 'that is not so: for the pope has summoned the land once, and if he summons it again, then, quoth he, it is lawful to rise against the queen and do it if she will not, for the pope is head of the Church.' " (*S. P. Dom.*, Eliz., Add. xv, 16).

Many of the leaders, however, were by no means prepared to adopt such an extreme measure as this. Northumberland himself with others, if we may believe his own story, shrank from the dishonour of treason which it would involve. A meeting at Topcliffe broke up in disorder upon this point, and the conspirators parted to wait for a more convenient season for action. But the course of events was too strong. When at length there was no alternative but to present themselves in person before the Council in London they hesitated no longer, but threw off the mask. On 14 November the Earls of Northumberland and Westmorland, with a great company,[9] were up in arms: their avowed purpose being to band together those of what they called "the old and catholic faith" for the redress of grievances, and to resist force by force.

With the events of the Northern Rebellion itself we are not immediately concerned.[10] It may suffice to say briefly that the revolt had been foreseen and to some

[9] The names of the gentlemen concerned are given by Laderchi (*Annales Ecclesiastici* ii, 315 f.).

[10] A brilliant though inaccurate account will be found in J. A. Froude, *History of England*, cap. liii (vol. ix, pp. 96–217, popular edition); see also Strype, *Annals*, chap. liv (vol 1, part ii, pp. 308–28, ed. Oxford, 1824). There is a good selection of documents, including the Bowes papers, in [Sir Cuthbert Sharpe] *Memorials of the Rebellion of 1569*, London, 1840. The second volume of the *State Papers* of Sir R. Sadler (Edinburgh, 1809) contains his correspondence as Treasurer of the Northern army; and the great collection in the Record Office is contained in the *State Papers, Domestic*, Elizabeth (Addenda, vols. xv, xvii). The fullest contemporary narratives are the account written by Thomas Bishop to the Council (Hatfield MS. 1490, given in substance in the *Calendar of Hatfield MSS.*, vol. i, p. 469 f.), and the *Answers to Interrogatories* made by the Earl of Northumberland in June 1572 (*S. P. Dom.* Eliz., Add. xxi, 56, 63). The Acts of the Privy Council from 3 May 1569 to 24 May 1570 are unfortunately missing (*Acts of the Privy Council*, N. S., vol. vii, pp. viii, 351).

extent provided for. At first indeed the rebels were masters of the situation; since the Queen's levies, very hastily and imperfectly drawn together and even worse provided with materials of war,[11] proved insufficient to meet them in the field. But before the end of December they had made "a fond and foolish end".[12] The Earl of Sussex hung upon their flank wherever they went; the country did not rise as they had been led to expect, and their own forces melted away rapidly. At length the two earls, with their immediate followers, were compelled to seek a precarious shelter amongst the Scottish border clans.

This, however, was not the end of the rebellion; for, as Lord Hunsdon at once wrote to Cecil, "although the upper skin of the wound be partly healed, the wound festers."[13] There was another who was far more dangerous than the two earls, both because he was more capable, and because his family was more loyally obeyed throughout the country-side than they.[14] Leonard Dacre (or Dacres) had been deeply implicated in the earlier rising, although he had not actually taken part in it. He remained at his castle of Naworth, ostensibly holding it for the Queen, in reality gathering his

[11] The State Papers are full of complaints on this score: see also *Correspondence diplomatique de la Mothe Fenelon*, tom. ii, p. 378.

[12] Sir Ralph Sadler to Cecil, 22 December: *S. P. Dom.*, Eliz., Add. xv, 119.

[13] *S. P. Dom.* Eliz., Add. xvii, 26: Berwick, 13 January.

[14] Again and again stress is laid upon this fact. See the letter of the Bishop of Carlisle quoted above. Lord Scrope writes to Sussex that the whole country, as well the gentry as others, "are addicted to a Dacre" (*S. P. Dom.* Eliz., Add. xvii, 37²), and again to Cecil that few will be found "to execute their force against a Dacre" (ibid., xvii, 56). Perhaps it is not unnatural that after the overthrow Hunsdon was able to write to the Council that he never heard a man "so cried out upon and cursed, both by men, women and children, as Leonard Dacre" (ibid., xvii, 110).

friends and making preparations. Early in February 1570 he was summoned to prove his loyalty by making his submission in person; whereupon he at once raised the standard of revolt. A very short delay would probably have placed him at the head of a force sufficient to enable him to meet any that could be sent against him. But the Queen's cousin, Lord Hunsdon, then Governor of Berwick, hastily collected such troops as he could and marched to Naworth. Finding Dacre too strong for him, he was hastening forward to effect a junction with Lord Scrope the Governor of Carlisle, when he was himself attacked by Dacre at daybreak of 20 February on the steep bank of the little river Gelt. Outnumbered as his forces were, exhausted with a long and difficult march, and with the disadvantage of position, Lord Hunsdon gained a brilliant victory.[15] Dacre was totally defeated, and fled across the border; and, excepting so far as the executions and confiscations were concerned, the revolt was at an end.

[15] On the importance of the battle of the Gelt, see Creighton, *Queen Elizabeth*, ed. 1899, p. 121.

III

BUT whilst we are not concerned to trace the course of the rebellion in detail, its general character certainly claims our attention. The fact is clear, and must be borne in mind, that it was distinctly of the nature of a crusade. The first step of the rebels had been to march upon Durham and break into the Cathedral, where they destroyed the Holy Table, tore in pieces the Bible and Service Books, and presently restored the Latin Service.[1] The following day, 15 November, the earls put forth their proclamation:

We Thomas Earle of Northumberlande and Charles Earle of Westm^rlande the quenes trewe and faithfull subiectes to all the same of the olde and catholique faithe: Knowe ye that we wth many other well disposed aswell of the nobility as others have promised our faithe to the furtheraũce of this o^r good meaninge. Forasmoch as diuẽse disordered and ill disposed p̄sons abowte the quenes ma^tie haue by ther craftie and subtill dealinge to aduaũce them self oũthrowen in this realme the trewe and catholique religion towardes God, and by the same abuseth the quene dishonẽth the realme & now lastly seketh to procure the destrucc̃on of this nobility: We therfore haue gathered o^r selfes together to resiste forse by forse and rather by the helpe of God [&] yo^u good

---

[1] Apparently this did not take place till about St Andrew's Day. For the ecclesiastical proceedings of the rebels and those who joined with them, see *Depositions and other Ecclesiastical Proceedings from the Courts of Durham*, Surtees Society, vol. xxi, pp. 127–205.

people to redresse these thinges amisse wth the restoringe of all ancient customes & Liberties to God & this noble realme, and lastly if we shall not doo it o^r selfes we might be reformed by strandgeres to the great hassarde of the state of this o^r coūtry wherevnto we are all bounde.

God save the queane.[2]

Nor did the movement ever lose its distinctively religious character. Wherever they went mass was said daily[3]; all their force wore red crosses,[4] and the leaders crucifixes of gold[5]; and the aged Richard Norton, who had been sheriff of Yorkshire, marched at their head

[2] *S. P. Dom.*, Eliz. xv, 29[1], a copy sent by the Council of the North to the Privy Council. It is given by Strype with certain inaccuracies, "as they were sent up from the Dean of York to Grindal" (*Annals*, 1, ii, p. 313). With this may be compared the summary in *S. P. Dom.*, Eliz., xv, 29[2]. In a later protestation sent by the rebel earls to Lord Derby on 26 November 1569, and by him communicated to the Council, they say nothing about religion. Whereas it was "faithfully and deliberately considered and advised" by the Duke of Norfolk and other noblemen, "with a common consent of sundry the principal favourers of God's Word", and this "godly good and honourable meaning of the said nobility hath been sought by all manner of means to be prevented by certain common enemies of the realm, near about the Queen Majesty's person", they have assembled themselves "to resist force by force " (Hatfield MS. 1419; *Burghley Papers* i, 564; Strype, *Annals*, 1, ii, 314).

[3] John Vaughan to Robert Owenson, 24 November: *S. P. Dom.*, Eliz., Add. xv, 37: "They haue masse dayly yet they do comytt grete spoyl dayly."

[4] Sir F. Leek to the Council, 3 December 1569: *S. P. Dom.*, Eliz., Add. xv, 73: "all theyre forsse bothe horse men and foote men do weyre redde crosses aswell the p̄stes [priests] as thothers." Lord Hunsdon caused his soldiers to wear the same sign before the attack on Leonard Dacre (Hunsdon and Foster to Scrope, 18 February 1570; ibid., xvii, 96[1]).

[5] See a very interesting letter from an unknown person (Matthew Hutton, Dean of York?) to Cecil: *S. P. Dom.*, Eliz., Add. xvii, 72.

bearing their banner with the emblems of the holy war.[6]

And the challenge was definitely accepted. As soon as trouble began to be anticipated, steps were taken to secure that all justices of the peace and other persons of importance in the country districts should subscribe a declaration promising to enforce the Act of Uniformity, and themselves to obey its provisions.[7] A prayer was published by authority, to be used in churches, for the quelling of the rebellion, as subsequently there was issued a thanksgiving that it had been suppressed with such ease.[8] In the North the cause of the Queen was to be definitely set forth as the cause of justice and of religious truth. A draft is extant, in Cecil's handwriting, of an instruction sent by the Council to the Earl of Sussex, the Queen's lieutenant-general in the North. In this the Council are made to say:

> Having called to our remembrance, how seditioosly

[6] Camden, *Annals*, p. 134, ed. 1630: "Trouping together vnder their Colours (wherein were painted in some the fiue wounds of Christ, in others the Chalice) Richard Norton an old gentleman with a reuerend gray head bearing a Crosse with a streamer before them." Hilles to Bullinger, 6 February 1570, mentions also "some banners of certain saints"; and Grindal to Bullinger, 18 February 1570, "the representation of a cross with this inscription, *In hoc signo vinces*" (*Letters from the Archives of Zurich*, pp. 330, 332); cf. also Stow, *Chronicle*, p. 663 (ed. 1615).

[7] See the declaration in Froude, ix, 116. A list of the justices of the peace in the English counties, endorsed in Cecil's hand "October 1569", was doubtless prepared for the purpose (*S. P. Dom.*, Eliz., lix, 14). After it, in November and December, there follow the certificates of the signature of the form by the justices of the various counties, etc.

[8] The former must have appeared in December 1569, the latter in January 1570; they are given in *Liturgical Services of the Reign of Queen Elizabeth*, Parker Society, pp. 536, 538; cf. p. 462. They were subsequently attached to the Homily of Wilful Rebellion. See *post*, p. 30.

the Rebels to furder their purpooses and to allure mul-
titud to them, doo, amongst other ther rebellioos
Attempts, pretend that they seke to have an alteration
of the religion, which in dede is stablished both by God's
Word, and by the laws of the Realme; and in place
therof do with hypocresy amongst the vulgar gross
people, cause certen lewd collations to be made in com-
mendation of the Pope, and the Mass and such lyke;
usyng also a Multitude of superstitioos cerymonies to
that end: We thynk it very necessarie, that such powre
of the Queens Majesties good subjects, as shall be
assembled to suppress those popish Treytors, being
sworn enemyes to God's truth and ther Contrey, should
contrary wyse be armed with God's Grace, my makyng
oppen profession of ther trew manner of service to God,
according to his Word, in all places, aswell therby to
provoke the assistance of God's ayde to them ageynst
his enemyes, as to confound the wycked and fals
Idolatry of the Rebells. And for this purpooss we thynk
it good, that your Lordship shuld gyve speciale and
express ordre: that dayly ther shuld be in severall placees
conuenient for the whole army, publick and common
Prayers used, such as we esteeme the Litany to be, so as
all Persons of all degrees shuld not miss, but once in the
daye at the lest, be present wher they might devoutly
heare the Litany: And specially to forsee that no cap-
tayns nor principall Officers do absent themselves; for
if any so shall doo without necessary cause, it shall not be
good to employ them in this Service. And we cold also
wish that some discrete Prechers were to attend uppon
your Lordship, that might at convenient Tymes,
specially uppon the holly Dayes, use some honest and
godly exhortations to the People in sondry places, to
moue them to serve God accordyng to his Command-
ments, and to be faythfull and trew to the Quenes
Majesty ther soverayn Lady, appoynted by Almighty
God to be their Ruler; of whom much good may be
truly spoken, thrugh God's goodnues, as of any Prince
that ever rayned over them, for her Clemency and
Mercy, and for hir Care and Love towards hir People.
And therwith may be with good rea son specially noted,

how these Traytors and Rebells ar to be of all good subjects abhorred; whom after so long a Peace in the Realme, and whylest God blessed us therin beyond all Nacions, the Devill hath styrred, as his Instruments, to be the authors of this inward Warr, and to provok bloodshed of ther Contry Men; wherof, Almighty God gyvyng the Quenes Majesty the strength of hir good Subjects, they shall shortly receave the dew Reward belongyng to Rebells. ... And thus having in this sort remembred your Lordship of this spirituall armyng yow and your Company, according to our bounden Duties, we meane not to be negligent in caryng for all other wordly thynges nedefull for your Strength, as thyngs or-dayned by God, to strengthen such as putt ther Trust in hym, ageynst his Enemyes, whom we trust shortly to see confounded.[9]

Sussex was not the man to let the manifesto of the Earls pass unanswered; and on 28 November he pub-lished a proclamation in the Queen's name, which, as he says,[10] was grounded upon theirs, and which traverses it point by point. Strype has given the sub-stance of some parts of this[11]; but on account of its interest and importance it is here reprinted, for the first time, from a copy in the British Museum:

A Proclamation set foorth by Therle of Sussex, the Queenes Maiesties Lieuetenaunt generale in the North, declaring truely the falsehodes and vayne delusions vvherby Therles of Northumberlande and VVestmer-

[9] Hatfield MS. 1425: printed in the *Burghley Papers*, i, 558. The instruction itself does not appear to be in existence; it must have been sent about 20 November, since it would appear that Sussex had re-ceived it before he issued his proclamation of 28 November.

[10] Sussex to Cecil, 30 November: *S. P. Dom.*, Eliz. Add. xv, 33. He sends a copy of the proclamation itself with the letter, but it is not there now. Perhaps it may have been detached and sent to the printers in order that it might be reprinted in London, as was certainly done.

[11] Strype, *Annals* 1, ii, p. 317 f.

lande, and their confederates, do abuse the Queenes Maiesties subiectes, to mayntayne their rebellious enterprises, the xxviii. of November 1569.

WHERE Therles of Northumberlande and Westmerlande with their confederates haue most vndutifully and vnnaturally conspired to leuie warre against their and our most gratious soueraine Lady the Queenes Maiestie, and thervpon haue entred into open and actuall rebellion, and to couer their wicked and detestable attemptes, haue abused and deluded many of her Maiesties subiectes in these partes, sometymes commaunding them in her highnesse name to repayre to them in warlike maner for the defence and suretie of her Maiesties person, when their intent of calling them was indeede to mainteine their horrible treasons, and therby to put in perill her most royall person, whom God long preserue, sometymes affirming their doynges to be with thaduise and consent of the nobilitie of this Realme, who in deede be wholly bent (as manifestly doth appeare) to spende their lyues in dutifull obedience against them and all other traytours, somtimes pretending for conscience sake to seeke to refourme religion, where in deede it is manifestly knowen many of them neuer had care of conscience, or euer respected any religion, but continued a dissolute lyfe, vntyll at this present they were driuen to pretende a popishe holynesse,[12] to put some false

[12] There can be no question that this estimate of the two leaders is substantially true. With it may be compared what was said of them in the proclamation put forth by the Queen at Windsor four days earlier: "As for reformation of any great matter, it is euident that they be as euyl chosen two persons (yf their qualities be well consydered) to haue credite, as can be in the whole Realme . . . beyng both in pouertie, the one hauing but a very small portion of that which his auncestors had and lost; and the other hauing almost his whole patrimonie wasted." (From the original of 24 November 1569, in the rare collection of Elizabethan Proclamations made by Humfrey Dyson in 1618, now No. 6463 in the Grenville Collection in the British Museum Library. The same thing, in a fuller form, is said by Thomas Norton in his tract addressed *To the Quenes Maiesties poore deceyued subiects of the North Countrey* (see *post*, p. 28). Cf., Jewel to Bullinger, 7 August 1570: "Two of our nobility indeed, young and

colour vpon their manifest treasons, directly against the
commaundement of God in holy scripture, the lawes
of this Realme, and the auncient prerogatiue of the
imperiall crowne of Englande, sometymes declaring that
they be driuen to take this matter in hande, lest other-
wyse forraine princes myght take it vpon them, to the
great perill of this Realme: where in deede they not
contented with the good quiet and publique administration of iustice, so long continued vnder the Queenes
Maiestie, as the lyke was neuer before in any princes
tyme, haue by all the wicked meanes they could, prac-
tised with forrayne princes to ayde them in this wicked
enterprise, and thereby sought not only the manifest
perill of our most gratious souerayne Ladyes person,
state and dignitie royall, but also to bryng the whole
Realme to perpetuall thraldom and miserie, vnder the
subiection and slauerie of forrayne powers and potentates, hoping therby to satisfie some part of their licentious and dissolute myndes, and sometymes couering
their naughtie intentes with a shewe of desire to preserue
the state of the auncient nobilitie from destruction, prepared (as they say) against them: where in deede it
manifestly appeareth, that in whole twelue yeres past the
Queenes Maiestie hath had such care of the preseruing
of that state, as from the beginning of her raigne to this
houre there hath not perished one of that flocke, and
they them selues who abuse the people with these slaun-

foolish and dissolute, who cared more for dice than for religion"
(*Letters from the Archives of Zurich*, p. 340). One of them is spoken
of much more severely in the tract *The Execution of Justice in
England not for Religion but for Treason*, which was put forth by
Lord Burghley about 1580: "As for some examples of the heads of
these rebellions, out of England fled Charles Nevill, Earl of Westmorland, a person utterly wasted by looseness of life, and by God's
punishment, even in the time of his rebellion, bereaved of his children that should have succeeded him in the earldom; and how his
body is now eaten of ulcers of lewd causes, all his companions do see,
that no enemy he had can wish him a viler punishment" (given in
Gibson, *Preservative from Popery*, ed. Cumming, vol. xvii, p. 49).
The words are those of a political enemy, but can hardly be devoid
of truth.

derous deuices, haue most gratiously and liberally tasted
of her Maiesties fauour, good countenaunce, bountie,
and familier vsage, more then other dyd of their equalles,
and farre aboue their desertes, and of whom her Maiestie
had conceaued so good opinion, as hardly coulde she of
long tyme he induced to thinke that either such lacke
of duetie coulde enter into their heartes agaynst their
souerayne, or such ingratitude against her that had so
liberally dealt with them, and so louingly vsed them,
although she manifestly knewe that some of them liued
in daunger of her lawes, whereof she gaue them to vnderstande she had good knowledge, and dyd tollerate with
them in hope of their loyalties otherwayes.

In consideration whereof, we Thomas Earle of Sussex,
her Maiesties Lieutenaunt generall in the north partes,
seeyng howe the ignoraunt people be abused by these
delusions, and knowyng what constaunt promises, asser-
tions, & othes they haue heretofore made by theyr owne
mouthes to the Queenes Maiestie, as also of late by her
Maiesties direction to vs to be reported to her highnesse
for the continuaunce of their truethes & loyalties to her
Maiestie: & seing by the sequel that all which heretofore
they haue done, or presently do, or hereafter intende to
do, be but fore pretended falshodes, to delude all states,
degrees and persons to serue their wicked purposes: haue
thought it conuenient hereby to notifie to al her
Maiesties subiectes their maner of dealinges, wherby
they may manifestly see, that their principal intentes
be to put in perill the person of our most gracious
soueraigne, whom God long preserue, to sowe sedition
and rebellion by all the false meanes they may, to do
their vttermost to put her Maiestie in daunger of her
most lawfull royall crowne and dignitie, to drawe
foreyne nations into this Realme, to the vtter subuertion
and perpetuall bondage of this auncient free common
wealth, to spoyle al kind of people, wherof the whole
countrey feeleth the present smart, and to mainteyne &
continue their licentious and vnbrideled affections, and
with falshodes, open lyes, and vayne delusions, to seeke
to abuse all kinde of states, for the furthering of their
wicked intentes, and prolonging of their detestable

doinges, which God of his justice can not long suffer to continue.

All whiche matter euidently appearing to the whole worlde, be sufficient to induce all men that haue either reason, duetie to the souerayne Ladie, or loue to their natiue countrey, and haue ben by these delusions abused, vtterly to forsake and detest them and their wicked doinges, and al such as haue not hitherto ben abused to forbeare to repayre to them, or any wayes to ayde or succour them or any of theirs in these traiterous enterprises, abhominable before God, vndutifull to their soueraine Ladie, and most perilous to the quiet and prosperous state of this Realme, where in honest persons haue lyued from the beginning of her Maiesties raigne in freedom of their persons, with suertie of lyfe, landes, and goodes, which God long continue.

God saue the Queene.[13]

T. Sussex.

[13] From the original in the Dyson Collection above referred to (Brit. Mus. G. 6463). The proclamation was reprinted in London by Richard Jugge and Cawood, but without their name (Arber, *Transcript of the Registers of the Company of Stationers*, v. 70). This is doubtless a copy of the reprint, as is shown by the title, which would not be found in the original published at York.

IV

We now turn to the measures which were taken by the authorities after the rebellion was over, and with a view to the future.

It is possible that Elizabeth never anticipated any great difficulties from this particular revolt, but she was evidently deeply moved by the fact that it had taken place at all, and by the instability of her position. Whether truly or not, she told the French ambassador that from the first she had expected it to come to nothing, and that she had left it alone in order that it might melt away by itself.[1] But as soon as it was safely over her fears made themselves manifest in the cruel vengeance which she took. Orders went forth for executions on a very large scale; a policy which, whilst it was suggested by several of the leaders of the Queen's forces,[2] caused no little dismay and disgust both amongst those who were called upon to execute her ruthless will, and in the realm as a whole.[3] Elizabeth's

[1] La Mothe Fenelon to the King of France, 17 December: "A quoy la dicta Dame avec grand affection m'a respondu . . . que quant à l'enterprinse des siens ce n'estoit que témérité, et qu'elle avoit layssé tout exprès déborder ces deux comtes, sans s'oposer beaulcoup à eulx du commancement, pour l'espérance de ce qui est despuys advenu, que eulx et toutz ceulx qui les favorisent sont desjà bien fort laz de leurs follyes, et s'en vont rompuz d'eulx mesmes." (*Correspondance diplomatique*, ii, 398.)

[2] E.g., by Sir Valentine Brown, *S. P. Dom.*, Eliz., Add. xv, 102.

[3] Something of this feeling may be traced in the language of the Thanksgiving, in which it is said that some of the seditous persons have been "most dreadfully scourged wth terrible executions, justly inflicted for their disobedience".

parsimony, born of her experiences in the past and of
her desire to place her realm in a good financial position, is notorious. As she had stinted her generals whilst
they were in the field, so now she took care to strike at
those who possessed property which might be con-
fiscated, whilst others less productive were allowed to
escape, unless they happened to be specially deeply
implicated. With characteristic selfishness, whilst she
omitted no precaution which might draw the disaffected to her, she showed herself suspicious and un-
grateful towards those who had served her best. The
flattering letter which she wrote to Lord Hunsdon
after his victory over Leonard Dacres is well known[4];
but the fact that she left him without any more sub-
stantial reward is no less notorious. There was one who
had served her even better: the sagacious and resource-
ful Earl of Sussex, who had borne the brunt of the
whole rebellion.[5] Sussex was not a courtier; and her
wayward inconsiderateness called forth from him at
length the following striking letter to Cecil:

> I was first a lieutenant: I was after little better than
> a marshal; I had then nothing left to me but to direct
> hanging matters (in the meantime all was disposed that
> was within my commission), and now I am offered to

[4] It is printed by Froude, *Hist. of England*, ix, 216.

[5] There is a curious and interesting tract in verse, *A Remem-
braunce of the Life Death and Vertues of . . . Thomas late Erle of
Sussex . . . The report of George Whetstones gent.* London, 1583. It
speaks as follows of the Rebellion (leaf 5 *recto*) :
  "Dismaid no whit, to heare this lowd *Allarme*,
  For wel he wist, that traytors had no might,
  Her *Highnesse* frends, and subiectes he did arme:
  And with a fewe, the *Rebels* put to flight:
  Yer [*ere*] that, the Princes power could come in sight.
  Without bloudshed, the broyle thus ended he,
  Saue such as died, by iustice on a tree."

be made a Sheriff's bailiff to deliver over possessions. Blame me not, good Mr Secretary, though my pen utter somewhat of a swell in my stomach, for I see I am kept but for a broom, and when I have done my office to be thrown out of the door. I am the first nobleman that hath been thus used. True service deserves honour and credit, and not reproach and open defaming; but seeing the one is ever delivered to me instead of the other, I must leave to serve or lose my honour; which being continued so long in my house, I would be loth should take blemish with me. These matters I know proceed not from lack of honourable meaning in the Queen's Majesty towards me, nor from lack of duty and truth in me towards her, which grieves me the more; and therefore, seeing I shall be still a camelion, and yield no other show than it shall please others to give the colour, I will content myself to live a private life. God send her Majesty others that mean as well as I have done; and so I commit you to the Almighty.

From Darnton, the 23rd of January, 1569[–70].

Yours assuredly,

T. SUSSEX.[6]

But whilst Elizabeth was showing the worst and most perverse side of her character in ways such as these, she and her great minister were projecting wise and far-seeing measures with a view to securing the loyalty of her people and commending her government to their consciences.[7]

---

[6] Hatfield MS. 1467; printed by E. Lodge, *Illustrations of British History*, i, 488, ed. 1838.

[7] The contemporary tracts and ballads upon the Northern Rebellion are such as to show that the loyalty of the Queen's subjects in the South did not stand in need of such a stimulus. They are very numerous, as may be seen in the lists of books, etc., entered at Stationer's Hall at the time (Arber, *Transcript of the Registers of the Company of Stationers*, i, 402–17); and extracts from three of the rimed pieces are given in the Parker Society's collection of *Select Poetry of the Reign of Elizabeth*, at pp. 542, 547, 549. Perhaps the most remarkable of them are two tracts which are described by Strype;

1. There exists in the Record Office a draft "Memorial of proceedings to be taken in the North", which seems to have been drawn up by Cecil in December 1569, as soon as it appeared that the revolt was nearing its end. Amongst its provisions are the following:

The vulgar people wold be tought, how this rebellion was pnicious [*pernicious*] to yᵉ Realme, and ageynst the honoʳ of God.

Wher so evʳ any bells wer rong to rayse rebellion, ther wold for a memory be left but on bell in yᵉ steple.[8]

Some notable exãple wold be made of ye prestes yᵗ have offended in this rebelliõ.[9]

To avoyd despatiõ [*desperation*] it wold be published yᵗ all psõs [*persons*] not allredy taken yᵗ will come and submitt thē selves, shuld be receaved, & vpon good

viz., *To the Quenes Maiesties | poore deceyued Subiectes of the North | Countrey, drawen into rebellion | by the Earles of Northum | berland and West | merland | Written by Thomas Norton | Seen and allowed according | to the Quenes Iniunctions | and ¶ A warnyng agaynst the | dangerous practises of the Papistes, | and specially the parteners of the | late Rebellion. | ¶ Gathered out of the common feare | and speche of good subiectes. | Vox populi Dei, vox Dei est. | Sene and allowed.* Of these the former was printed by Bynne-man in 1569, and the latter by Day without date but early in 1570; and two editions of each appeared. Strype rightly calls attention to the importance of these contemporary documents, and gives large extracts from both of them (*Annals*, chap. lv, vol. 1, part ii, pp. 328–44). But he appears to have seen only mutilated copies, and says that the former "by the style, strength, and spirit of it seems to be composed by the head and pen of Sir Thomas Smith", who afterwards succeeded Cecil as Secretary. As a matter of fact they are both (the latter as appears by the title page of the second edition) the work of the well-known laywer and playwright, Thomas Norton, who trans-lated Dean Nowell's *Longer Catechism* into English (see the Parker Society's edition, p. viii).

[8] This is worthy of note, and may be the cause of not a few rifled steeples in the border counties and the Bishopric.

[9] One recusant priest, Plumtree by name, was hanged at Durham in pursuance of this plan. See Camden, *ubi supr.*

suertyes to be forth cōmȳg should remaȳ out of p̄son untill they shuld obteyn hir Mat^ys p̄dō [*pardon*][10]

2. With this may be compared the instructions issued by the Queen to the Earl of Sussex and his fellow Commissioners for dealing with those who had been concerned in the subsequent revolt under Leonard Dacre.[11] Amongst other instructions is one which directs that, before receiving the submission of any person:

> You shall cawse their repentance to be manifestly seen by their submission and confession of their horrible crymes, and to thintent they may be the redier to acknowledg the same, It shall do well, that at certen dayes mete for the purpose there may be Instructions given them by some discrete prechers in open sermons, to the wch they may be directed to resort before they shall appear before you, and there be tought to know their synes against Almighty God, and their offences agaynst us.[12]

[10] *S. P. Dom.*, Eliz., Add. xv, 39.

[11] The proclamation of pardon to those concerned in Dacre's revolt, dated Hampton Court, 4 March (*S. P. Dom.*, Eliz., Add. xviii, 4), is strikingly moderate compared with those which had gone before. It declares, as was the case, that the Queen's subjects had been "abused and falsly allured to ayde him," partly for defence of his possession which he had gotten of certen houses wherevnto he pretended title . . . and partly to w^tstand certen incursions that he vntruly pretended shuld be shortly made into those borders by the outlawes of Scotland and the rebells lately fledd out of England"; and goes on to say that "the multitude of hir said poore subjects . . . have most lamentably acknowledged and confessed their errors and w^t clamors and outcryings have accursed the said Leonard Dacres as a most wicked and pnitious trayter, making most pitifull intercessions . . . that they might be receaved to hir Matys mercy and haue their pardons, w^t full intent to be hereafter during their lyves more carefull how to be abused in like māner to assemble & arme theselves upon provocatiō of any privat subiect hauing no office nor authority vnder hir Mat^y, as in dede the said Leonard Dacres had none."

[12] *S. P. Dom.*, Eliz., Add. xviii, 7.

3. The provision for "Instructions by discreet preachers" may have suggested a further step which was taken not long afterwards, viz., the preparation by the ecclesiastical authorities of a homily on rebellion, to be used both then and afterwards as occasion might require. Such a homily had been projected by Cranmer after the rebellion in the West in 1549; and the notes which he drew up for the purpose are still extant.[13] The project was now taken in hand by Archbishop Parker, doubtless with the assistance of others[14]: and the result was the lengthy "Homily against Disobedience and Wilful Rebellion", with its well-known warning:

> Let no good and discreet subjects therefore follow the flag or banner displayed to rebellion, and borne by rebels, though it have the image of the plough painted therein, with *God speed the plough* written under in great letters, knowing that none hinder the plough more than rebels, who will neither go to the plough themselves, nor suffer others that would go unto it. And though some rebels bear the picture of the five wounds painted, against those who put their only hope of salvation in the wounds of Christ—not those wounds which are painted in a clout by some lewd painter, but in those wounds which Christ himself bare in his precious body —though they, little knowing what the cross of Christ meaneth, which neither carver nor painter can make, do bear the image of the Cross painted in a rag, against those that have the cross of Christ painted in their hearts; yea, though they paint withal in their flags, *Hoc signo vinces*, "By this sign thou shalt get the victory", by a most fond imitation of the posy of Constantinus Magnus, that noble christian emperor and great conqueror of God's enemies, a most unmeet ensign for rebels, the enemies of God, their prince and country, or what other banner

[13] Cranmer, *Remains and Letters*, Parker Society, p. 188.
[14] Strype discerns signs of Parker's own hand in the Thanksgiving (*Annals* 1, ii, 322); but they are also abundant elsewhere.

soever they shall bear, yet let no good and godly subject, upon any hope of victory or good success, follow such standard-bearers of rebellion.[15]

The Homily in six parts,[16] together with the Prayer and Thanksgiving already mentioned, was published late in 1570 or early in 1571.[17] Directions were speedily given that it should be placed in all parish churches,[18] and in 1574 it was included in the Second Book of Homilies.[19]

4. But by far the most important of the documents called forth by the rebellion is the noble *Declaration of the Queen's Proceedings since her Reign*, which is here reprinted. In it Elizabeth sets forth at length the principles upon which her whole government had been based, first as regards civil affairs, and then as regards religion. In each respect she affirms that there is no breach with the past, that nothing novel, extravagant, or unwarranted has taken place; in each respect, on the other hand, she boldly challenges a comparison be-

[15] From the Fourth Part. (*The Homilies*, ed. Corrie, p. 583, f.)
[16] They were sometimes regarded as distinct homilies, and the prayer is to be used after each. The fourth part was printed at the end of a Form of Prayer issued for King Charles I at Oxford, by Leonard Litchfield, the University printer, in 1643.
[17] The original edition of "¶An Homilie agaynst disobedience and wylful rebellion" was published by Jugge and Cawood. It is in quarto and without date; but it had certainly appeared by April 1571. It is now very scarce, but there is a copy in the Lambeth Palace Library (xxx, 3, 20).
[18] The Canons of 1571 direct that "the holy Homilies, which lately were written agaynst rebellion, be in euery church" (see the *Canons of 1571 in English and Latin*, Church Historical Society, No. XL), and Grindal, in his Injunctions for the Province of York of the same year, directs that there shall be provided in every church "the two tomes of the Homilies, with the Homilies lately written against rebellion" (Grindal, *Remains*, Parker Society, p. 133).
[19] In the edition published by Jugge and Cawood in that year.

tween her government and that of her predecessors.
Meantime she lays stress upon the fact that it was no
part of her policy to coerce men's consciences.[20] And on
this basis she appeals to her people to judge between
her government and those who are sowing sedition
within her realm. This candid, reasonable, and well-
balanced document will compare favourably with any
apology in English history; and it is, as the Bishop of
London has said, a complete answer by anticipation to
the bull *Regnans in excelsis* which was presently put
forth by Pius V.[21]

Curiously enough, we have no actual evidence (so
far as the present writer is aware) that this manifesto
ever reached the generation for whom it was intended.
It was evidently written after the first rebellion was
over, and before the outbreak of that under Leonard
Dacre; that is to say, in January 1570.[22] This latter no
doubt caused it to be delayed, and would have necessi-
tated further alterations. But it may even have caused
the *Declaration* to be forgotten altogether, or to be considered inopportune: for there does not appear to be
any printed copy of it now extant, nor even direct evidence that it ever was published in Elizabeth's lifetime.

It has been printed once, however, at least in sub-
stance; for it was included by Haynes in his collection
of Burghley *State Papers*, published more than a cen-

[20] Compare with this the order made in the Court of Star Chamber
on 15 June following. It is given in the Appendix, No. II.

[21] M. Creighton, *Queen Elizabeth*, ed. 1899, pp. 133–136. It is
there quoted from Cecil's draft as printed in the *Burghley Papers*.

[22] It is evident from the document itself (see p. 35) that it was
written between the two rebellions. A note at the end of the copy
in the Record Office, made by the late Mr R. Lemon and bearing
his initials, suggests February 1570 as its date on this ground; but
January is far more likely.

tury and a half ago.[23] It was there given however from the original draft amongst the MSS. at Hatfield House[24]; a draft which is evidently the work of Cecil himself, and has many alterations and additions in his handwriting. Of this there is a fair copy, somewhat revised, in the Record Office,[25] with very numerous emendations, many of which are highly characteristic, in the handwriting of Queen Elizabeth herself. It is this latter which is here printed, the alterations in the Queen's handwriting being given at the side of the page. For purposes of convenience the spelling is modernized, but Elizabeth's corrections are given *verbatim.*

[23] *A Collection of State Papers . . . transcribed from the Original Letters and other authentick Memorials . . . left by William Cecill Lord Burghley and now remaining at Hatfield House. . . .* By Samuel Haynes, A.M.; folio, London, 1740. The Declaration is at p. 589.

[24] Hatfield MS. 1450. It is described in the *Calendar of Hatfield MSS.* Issued by the Historical MSS. Commission, vol. i. p. 456.

[25] *S. P. Dom.* Eliz. vol. lxvi, no. 54.

A DECLARATION OF THE QUEEN'S PROCEEDINGS SINCE HER REIGN[1]

WHEN we consider with ourselves, how it hath pleased Almighty God of his abundant goodness to bless his good[a] creatures our subjects in all our dominions with such a general quietness and peace, as the like hath not been seen[b] in these our kingdoms in[c] many ages[d], until this last year (which was after the time of eleven full years of our Reign), that an[e] unnatural commotion of certain of our subjects in a part of our Realm in the North was by certain lewd practices of some few[f] secretly stirred up; and yet by God's goodness, with the faithfulness[g] of our true subjects[h], shortly suppressed and quieted[i]:

[a] *omit* good

[b] *om.* seen
[c] *om.* in
[d] *add* past

[e] on

[f] *add* seditious persons
[g] *add* and constancy
[h] *add* very
[i-i] without [bloodshed][2] any fight ended[3]

---

[1] The title only occurs as the endorsement of the draft amongst the Burghley Papers.

[2] Words in square brackets are written but crossed through in Elizabeth's hand.

[3] Elizabeth could hardly say that it had been suppressed "without bloodshed" after the executions which had taken place under her orders. But the ease with which the revolt had been overcome is again and again mentioned. See the *Homily on Rebellion*, part vi (ed. Corrie, p. 597): "God of his mercy miraculously calmed that raging tempest . . . almost without any shedding of Christian and English blood at all." And Grindal to Bullinger, 18 February 1570: "Thus was the rebellion suppressed within forty days, and without bloodshed, except that five hundred of the rebels were afterwards executed," etc. (*Letters from the Archives of Zurich*, Parker Society, p. 332.)

We find it necessary that, as we are most bound to render unto the same our good God the whole praise and honour for[j] these His[k] blessings[l] upon us and our dominions[m], and for the same[n] to continue[o] thankful; so ought we also, in respect of our princely charge[p], to consider both how this[q] interruption of the course of so universal long and continual inward peace hath happened; and how also by God's favour and assistance it may be provided that the like occasions hereafter be not ministered by seditious persons, whose nature cannot, nor as yet doth, [r]cease[r] to imagine and contrive secret means to [s]make[s] alteration of the[t] quietness, whereunto [u]of His[u] goodness our realm is now restored.[4]

And therefore, whereas it hath[v] appeared unto us, that although in some part there wanted not external incitements and provocations to animate and stir our people to withdraw their natural duties from us [w]and our laws[w], and to enter into rebellions; yet could not the same so have prevailed, if there had not been also therewith joined secret practices[x] of other malicious[y] persons, [z]partly being our subjects born and partly[z] residing within our realm; [a]who had cunningly and with colourable untruths[a], first [b]inveigled[b] some few of our nobility, [c]as the

j *add* all

k *add* singular
l *add* poured
m people
n *add* both we and they
o *add* allwise
p *add* and office
q *add* sudden

r–r altogether cease falsely
s–s breed some new
t *add* present
u–u by God's

v *add* well

w–w their sovereign

x *add* and drifts
y *om.* malicious
z–z *omit*
a–a [by whose covert interest and][5] for whose purposes to be brought to effect colourable devices were used
b–b to inveigle

---

[4] Burghley draft: "is now again restored".

same exceeded not two,[6] with[c] a false fear
of our indignation towards them, even
when in deed we did certainly and very
well favour and allow of them[d]; And [e]next,
that abused another sort and greater number[e] with false persuasions of some general
severity, intended by us and our ministers
against them, [f]only[f] in respect of opinions
in religion, when no[g] such thing did
appear, or was any wise by us meant or
thought of; and lastly, [h]enticed the[h] vulgar
and common sort[i] to fancy some novelties
and changes of laws and rulers, as the
ordinary[j] high[k] way to all sensual[l] and un-
ruly liberty, which commonly the ignorant[m] covet, though it ever[n] hath [o]been and
will be[o] most of all to their own[p]
destruction.

For these causes, thus manifestly
appearing to us, [q]notwithstanding that[q]
the whole course of our actions in our
government, from the beginning of our
Reign, if they were observed and reduced
unto memory, might serve to teach and
certify all sorts of our subjects to understand, and beware hereafter[7] of such blind
inveiglings, crafty abusings, and perilous
enticements of our people as indeed [r]the

c–c which took
effect in two
only, to bring
them into

d *add* both
e–e therewith
also for the
furtherance of
the same dan-
gerous purposes
it was [desired
to abuse][5] de-
vised colourably
to abuse a[n
other number]
certain number
of gentlemen
adhering to the
said two noble
men
f–f and that most
specially
g *add* token of
any
h–h to confirmate
this wicked
intention, there
lacked not
covert whisper-
ing to entice a
i *add* of [the
mean][8] people
j *add* pernicious
k *om.* high
l *add* beastly
m *add* people
most
n *om.* ever
o–o proved and
so always will
p *add* ruin and
q–q and other
like seditious
practices con-
joined with
them which we
do forbear to
specify,
although
r–r [we did well
prove][8]

---

[5] Words in square brackets are written but crossed through in Elizabeth's hand.

[6] Burghley draft: "inveigled two of our nobility (the sum so few as the same exceeded not two)".

[7] Burghley draft: "and to beware hereafter".

[8] Words in square brackets are written but crossed though in Elizabeth's hand.

s-s *omit*
t-t *portion of the country*
u-u *that small number which was thus abused did occupy*
v *add it may well appear that none did forget their duties*
w-w *the heads and [strivers of]^s stirrers of this rebellion*
x *add in other places*
y *add manifest.*
z *add unto us*
a *add and fidelity*
b-b *without exception of any one*
c-c *the [prayers and]^s humble and personal ready repair to us [and sending to us in their persons] of the greatest number [with offer of service], and of the rest either by actual service in the field, or in the countries where they had governance, but also of the universal readiness and earnestness*
d *add of every state*
e *add goods their bodies and*
f *unnatural*
g-g *comfort*
h *add satisfy and*
i *add practices and*
j-j *be plainly though briefly*
k *add of all sorts*
l *add all*
m-m *craftily imagined*
n *add hereafter*
o *add in our government*
p-p *saving only to such as by their open contempt and disobedience*
q-q *provoke us*

same did so work universally[r] in all other parts of our realm [s]by proof of the constancy and willing service of all the rest of our subjects, both noble and others[s], saving only that [t]small portion[t] which [u]our rebels occupied[u] by force[v]: For that when most avaunts were vainly made by [w]our rebels[w], that great numbers both of our nobles and commons[x] were confederated and would take part with them, there was[y] good proof made[z], not only of the constancy[a] of all the rest of our nobility [b]in all other parts of our realm, both[b] by [e]their deeds and words; but of the readiness[o] of all the other of our subjects[d] to serve us with their[e] lives against that small[f] portion of the rest that were stirred to rebel: Yet of our abundant goodness toward the [g]quiet state[g] of our good subjects, and for the desire we have by some public admonitions to[h] stay all sorts from the danger to be hereafter seduced and abused with such like [i] untruths, We will that it [j]shall[9] be briefly[j] understood[k], both what[l] our former intentions have been in our government platt contrary to the untrue reports [m]invented[m] and secretly scattered by malicious seditious and traitorous persons; and what course we intend[n] by God's grace to hold[o] towards all persons, [p]except by contrary behaviour and contempt of any of our subjects, we[p] shall [q]be induced[q] to make alteration therein.

[9] Burghley draft: "it be briefly understood".

First, we do all persons to understand that of our own natural disposition (through God's[r] goodness) we have been always desirous to have the obedience of all our subjects of [s]all sorts[s], both high and low[t], by love and not by compulsion, by their own yielding, and not by our exacting; Allowing that which was well said by a wise prince of[u] the Greeks: [v]"That king[v] to be in most surety that so ruled over his[w] subjects as [x]a natural[10] father over the[x] children."[11] And therefore [y]by God's grace[y] we may boldly [z]say[z] that there is no one example in our whole dominions to be produced that we ever by any means sought the life, the blood, the goods, the houses, states or lands of any person in[a] any estate[b] or degree, nor yet procured or suffered any division or discord to be stirred or maintained betwixt our nobility amongst themselves, or betwixt[c] one estate and another[d], for any our own avenge, profit, or [e]pleasure[e]: matters not otherwise to be remembered by ourselves, but [f]with humble thanks[f] to acknowledge [g]these blessings to be the mere gifts of God[g], and [h]therewith to declare the rare felicity of our time, and[h] to retain the continuance of our subjects' love towards us, to the honour of Almighty God[i], and to the maintenance of common tranquillity in our Realm.

[r] add specia

[s-s] every sort

[t] add to be assured to us

[u] amongst

[v-v] those kings

[w] their

[x-x] natural fathers did over their

[y-y] omit

[z-z] affirm and by God's sufferance rejoice

[a] of

[b] add condition

[c] add any

[d] other

[e-e] other respect

[f-f] in humble manner thankfully

[g-g] all these to proceed merely and only of Almighty God

[h-h] consequently by commemoration hereof against the malitious depravation of our estate

[i] add to the confusion and shame of the seditious so r t,

---

[10] Burghley draft: "as a father".

[11] I have not been able to trace the reference here.

And notwithstanding this our natural and private dulceness[j], yet we have not, [k]for the[k] public, and [l]for conservation of common peace, [m]and law[m], mutually betwixt our subjects of all estates, neglected to our power the due and direct administration of[n] justice for the suppressing of[o] malefactors in all particular[p] criminal causes; having also therewith had careful consideration[q] to diminish and avoid the multitude of such offenders[r], wherewith this age generally in all countries [s]aboundeth[s], in such sort as [t]by records may appear[t] that the Judges criminal of our Realm have in no [u]time[u] given fewer bloody judgements. In other causes that have been commonly[v] aforetimes, and are to be seen [w]in[w] this time [x](the more to be lamented) offensive[x] in some monarchies; as in[y] wasting of all sorts of people by [z]wilful and[z] continual[a] wars either foreign or civil, or in impoverishing of the subjects by perpetual and new devised [b]assizes, taxes[b], gabels, or such other exactions: We would[c] it were well and justly considered[d] that first, we never yet began war with any Prince or Country,[12] neither used force and arms but defensive, and not those at any time until such evident necessity (though [e]not seen to[e] the vulgar

---

[12] Compare Jewel on 1 Thess. v. 10 (*Works*, Parker Society, ii, 873): "This is the first disturbance and breach of that blessed peace in which God hath so long and so quietly preserved this realm, since that time that her Majesty came to the crown."

Marginal notes:

[j] *add* which in some Governments and some times might be misliked,
[k-k] in
[l] *om.* and
[m-m] *omit*
[n] *add* laws and
[o] *add* offenders and
[p] *add* both civil and
[q] *add* from time to time by laws and orders
[r] *add* as
[s-s] is troubled
[t-t] we think it may appear by records
[u-u] age before
[v] *add* offensive
[w-w] lamentably at
[x-x] *omit*
[y] *add* unmerciful
[z-z] *omit*
[a] *add* bloody
[b-b] taxes, assizes
[c] wish
[d] *add* and kept in memory
[e-e] these not so understood of

sort) compelled us[f] either to prevent, or defend[g] foreign forces levied to the manifest danger of our Realm, as without such provisions[h] it was manifest that notable invasions had been made into the[i] Realm both by land and sea, and those so dangerous as no man's judgement can[j] comprehend[k]. In[l] execution whereof, whatsoever extraordinary charges our good subjects either privately in service with their bodies, or commonly in[m] contributions [n]by subsidies, or such like, which as we know hath not been small, so[n] yet [o]neither[o] so frequent nor[p] grievous as [q]hath been[q] in[r] sundry our [s]progenitors' times, even to maintain[s] wars abroad[t], sought[u], and long continued without necessity. [v]Manifest[v] also it is, that [w]we have[w] of our own proper domain and revenues of our Crown[x], not forborne to expend that which hath been both honourable and necessary; and[y] the successes of these enterprises being well considered, none can justly say, that the Realm hath lost any[z] honour or interest thereby. We[a] leave to all [b]good and[b] wise [c]persons to consider by way of comparison,[13] what difference is to be found betwixt the security, the tranquillity, the wealth, and all other worldly

[f] *add* with the same
[g] repel
[h] *add* and God's special favour assisting the same
[i] this
[j] *add* yet
[k] *add* what might have been the event thereof
[l] *add* the progress and
[m] by
[n–n] have sustained, wherein [though they have been not very small] surely we have been for them very [grateful] yea sometime more grateful than we did deign to accept
[o–o] have they not been either
[p] or
[q–q] *omit*
[r] *add* the times of
[s–s] progenitors, for maintenance of foreign
[t] *add* directly
[u] *add* begun
[v–v] or any evident profit to this Crown. And manifest
[w–w] *omit*
[x] *add* which otherwise we have had special care always to conserve, we have
[y] *add* we trust
[z] *add* piece of
[a] Besides this we
[b–b] *omit*
[c] *add* and indifferent

[13] See the beginning of Thomas Norton's tract, *A Warning to the Queen's Majesty's Subjects* (see p. 28): "Compare the time of her most noble and gracious government with ages long ago past, and especially with the miserable and dangerous days immediately preceding her most happy and comfortable reign; call to memory the weakness and perils wherein the commonwealth stood before her

d *add* obedient
e *add* in this our government
f *add* in other kingdoms and countries
g *add* outrage
h *add* murders
i-i depopulations of towns and countries and therewith infinite manners of exaction
j-j *omit*
k-k heartily wish and desire
l-l wheresoever they be to the honour
m *add* the tranquility of Christendom, and to the maintenance of all due obedience to Princes and Governors
n-n There remaineth yet
o *add* specially from abroad
p *add* and maliciously
q-q by directing
r *add* Almighty
s *add* the
t *add* faith and
u *add* outward

v *add* unjustly

w-w the manifest
x *add* Almighty
y-y the duty of their Christianity
z *add* unnaturally to us and

felicities, which our[d] people do and may enjoy[e], and the contraries[f]; as continual and universal[g] bloodsheds[h], burnings, spoilings, [i]murders, exactions[i], and such like, properly conjoined with civil wars [j]in other countries[j]; all which we [k]wish[k] to cease, [l]through the mercies[l] of Almighty God[m].

[n]It remaineth further[n] to be considered (which is by divers[o] most frequently[p] impugned) what we have done to give occasion of offence and slanderous reports in the ordering of our Realm and people, [q]to cause[q] them to live in the fear and service of[r] God, and in the profession of[s] Christian[t] religion. Of which matter because in some things the Ecclesiastical external policy of our Realm by laws differeth from some other countries, as always there hath been in such[u] things a difference, occasion is sought, specially from foreign parts[v], to deprave this part of our government, and consequently by secret troubling the weak consciences of our people with untruths, to withdraw them from obedience of us and our laws; yea, from [w]all[w] divine service of[x] God, contrary to[y] their natural birth, and duty towards God[y] and[z] their native country.

highness coming to the crown; weigh the benefits, both bodily and ghostly, that the whole realm and all her subjects have, and do daily receive through her means; think upon the grievous and unspeakable miseries that we all shall be like to sustain by loss of her invaluable presence." This is flattery, but it has a solid basis of fact.

And in this part we would it were indifferently understood that whatsoever is [a]untruly reported, by words or writings of malicious and seditious persons, We know no other authority, either given or used by us, as Queen and Governor of this Realm, than hath been by the laws of God and this Realm always[b] due to our progenitors, sovereigns and kings of the same[c]; Although true it is that [d]this authority[d] hath been in the time of certain of our noble progenitors some hundred years past, as by laws, records, and stories doth appear (and specially in the Reign of our[e] noble father King Henry the viij[th] and our[f] dear brother King Edward the vj[th]) more clearly recognized[g] by all the estates of the [h]Realm[h], as the like hath been in our time; without that thereby we do either challenge or take to us (as malicious persons do untruly surmise) any superiority to [i]ourselves[i] to define decide or determine any article or point of the Christian faith and religion, or to change any ancient[j] ceremony of the Church from the form before received and observed by the Catholic and Apostolic Church, or [k]the use of[k] any function[l] belonging to any ecclesiastical[m] person[n] being a minister of the Word and[o] Sacraments in the Church. But that authority which is [p]yielded to us and[p] our Crown [q]consisteth in[q] this; that, considering we are by God's grace[r] the Sovereign Prince and Queen[s] next under

[a] *add* in this matter

[b] *add* annexed to the Crown of this realm and
[c] as by good sufficient and ancient authorities is to be proved
[d-d] the same

[e] *add* most

[f] *add* most
[g] *add* to the Imperial Crown
[h-h] same in parliament

[i-i] our self

[j] *add* rite or
[k-k] that we do challenge or use
[l] *add* or office
[m] *add* prelate or
[n] *add* of what degree soever
[o] or
[p-p] annexed to
[q-q] we take to be
[r] *add* and by lawful succession
[s] *add* of this realm immediately

t *add* born
u *om.* born
v-v other earthly ruler
w *add* this
x *add* very
y *add* and continued therein as one of the principal kingdoms of Christendom
z-z in duty to God to provide that
a should
b *add* and observation
c-c those ends
d justly
e *add* pastors
f *add* such other ecclesiastical
g-g and curates as by
h-h used in
i-i hath been in former ages ordained. Whom also we know that our duty is to assist with the power which God hath given us as they being the ministers of the Church, may according to the law of God, and the true rules and articles of our Christian faith retain our people in obedience to their Almighty God and to live as Christians to the salvation of their souls which Christ hath redeemed.
j *add* belonging
k *om.* due
l principally
m-m both in name and deed from the best of
n-n who when they do their best take only

God, and all the people[t] in our realm are immediately born[u] subjects to us and our Crown and to none [v]else[v], and that[w] our Realm hath of[x] long time past received the Christian faith[y], We are by this authority bound [z]to direct[z] all estates, being subject to us, to[a] live in the faith and the obedience[b] of Christian religion, and to see the laws of God and man which are ordained to [c]that end[c] to be duly observed, and the offenders against the same duly[d] punished, and consequently to provide, that the Church may be governed and taught by archbishops, bishops[e], and[f] ministers [g]according to[g] the ecclesiastical ancient policy [h]of[h] the realm, [i]whom we do assist with our sovereign power, &c.[i] An office and charge[j] as we think properly due[k] to all Christian monarchs, and princes sovereigns, whereby they only[l] differ [m]from[m] pagan princes, [n]that only take[n] care of their subjects' bodies[o] without respect to the salvation of their souls, or of the[p] life hereafter[q] to come. So as certainly no just occasion can hereby be taken to deprave our government in [r]any[r] causes ecclesiastical. And yet to answer further [s]all[s] malicious untruths[t] dispersed abroad to [u]induce[u] a grudging[v] of our government [w]in this behalf[w], we [x]know not, nor have[x] any meaning [y]to allow[y] that

o *add* and earthly lives
p any
q *add* immortally
r-r this sort in
s-s to some other
t *add* depending hereupon
u-u procure and nourish
v *add* against this manner
w-w *omit*
x-x affirm that we never had
y-y or intent

any our subjects should be[z] molested either[a] by examination or inquisition in any matter, either of[b] faith, as long as they shall profess the Christian faith[c], not gainsaying the authority of the holy Scriptures [d]and of[d] the articles of our faith contained in[e] the Creeds [f]Apostolic and Catholic[f]; or for [g]matter of ceremonies, or any other external matters[g] appertaining to Christian religion, as long as they shall in their outward conversation show them selves quiet and conformable, and not manifestly repugnant and obstinate to the laws [h]of the Realm[h], which are established [i]for frequentation of divine service in the[i] ordinary churches, [j]in like manner as all other laws are, whereunto subjects are of duty and by allegiance bound[j].

And if any potentate in Christendom,[14] challenging an universal and sole superiority over the whole Church of Christ (as it is[k] pretended)[l] shall condemn or reprehend this our [m]office appertaining and by justice[m] annexed to our Crown, because

[z] *add* troubled or
[a] *om.* either
[b] *add* their
[c] *add* in
[d–d] nor denying
[e] *add* any of
[f–f] received and used in the Church
[g–g] their opinion in any rites and ceremonies

[h–h] *omit*
[i–i] by the whole realm for resorting to their
[j–j] or places of common prayers, and using there of divine services

[k] *add* injuriously
[l] *add* without universal consent of all princes for their private dominions
[m–m] authority

---

[14] The passage which follows is, as the Bishop of London has said (*Queen Elizabeth*, p. 136, ed. 1899), an answer by anticipation to the claim made by Pius V in the Bull *Regnans in excelsis*: "He that reigneth on high, to whom is ascribed all power both in heaven and earth, hath committed the absolute government of his One, Holy, Catholic, and Apostolic Church, outside of which there is no salvation, to one only upon earth, namely to Peter, the Chief of the Apostles, and to Peter's successor the Bishop of Rome. Him alone he has made Prince, over all nations and kingdoms, to pluck down, destroy, scatter, consume, plant and build: that he may preserve the faithful, knit together in one common bond of charity, in the unity of the spirit, and present them safe and sound to their Saviour."

n *add* pretended
o–o impeach that same
p–p directly the only
q challenge
r *add* also
s *add* and were most requisite to be now put in execution
t *add* responsible
u–u and Christian answer
v *add* and shall be meet for a Christian monarch
w *add* of all estates Christian
x–x otherwise
y conform
z–z to that which
a *add* unto for the advancement of the Christian faith and concord of Christendom
b–b *omit*
c–c to be that which
d–d in peaceable manner
e–e that which is or shall be disguised and
f *add* to be received only
g–g *omit*
h–h motion of wars and rebellions or by
i *add* such
j *add* tyrannous
k *add* altogether contrary to Christian charity and altogether
l anything belonging to
m–m desperations, changes or alterations at the sensual appetites and vain imaginations of inordinate prelates

it is not derived from his[n] authority, We shall be ready in place and time convenient, where such person as shall so °reprehend us° may not be ᵖtheᵖ Judge of his own cause[q] (an order against nature) and where[r] other Christian monarchs, potentates, and princes shall be suffered generally to assemble with good freedom security and liberty, as in former better times hath been christianly used, to the great benefit of the Church of God[s], to cause such a[t] plain ᵘaccountᵘ to be made for our defence by the rules of Christian religion[v], as we trust shall in reason satisfy the university of the good and faithful[w]: Or ˣif notˣ, we shall be ready as the humble servant[15] and handmaid of Christ, to reform[y] our selves and our policy ᶻin any manner, asᶻ truth shall guide and lead us[a]. Which truth is to be ᵇby usᵇ understood known and received ᶜasᶜ Almighty God shall please to reveal ᵈit by his ordinary meansᵈ, and not to be ᵉin a disguised mannerᵉ obtruded and forced[f] by ᵍoutward force of wars, orᵍ threatenings of bloodshed or ʰsuch likeʰ curses fulminations or[i] other worldly[j] violences and practices: Things[k] unfit to be used for stablishing or reforming of[l] Christian religion, and to be rather contemned by sovereign princes, having their seats and thrones established by Almighty God, and not subject to ᵐthe

---

[15] Burghley draft: "as an humble servant".

wills of foreign and strange usurped potentates[m].

Thus, for things past[n], it may appear in[o] what [p]sort our mild, merciful, and reasonable government[p] hath been falsely and maliciously depraved [q]by seditious and obstinately ignorant persons[q]; whereupon all others[r] not yet incurably or deeply infected with [s]their[s] false[t] persuasions may[u] discern into what gross and lamentable errors all such our people have been [v]induced, as being herewith deceived[v], have been led[w] from their[x] obedience due to us by the laws of God and man, to commit treasons or[y] rebellions, and to adhere to external and strange power, having no interest in their persons by laws divine or human. And [z]now[z], that the craftiness of these seditious and pernicious persons may not hereafter again newly abuse the rest of our good subjects, as with new devisings untruly of things to follow, we do[a] all manner of persons to understand that, considering we well now at length perceive that some sorts[b] of our people of their nature are grown the worse and more disobedient or wanton by a general[c] opinion conceived of our lenity, we must and will for [d]redress thereof, against[d] such [e]being[e] manifestly[f] disobedient against us and our laws, proceed[g] with the Sword of Justice which God hath given us, and which we are charged not to bear in vain: Assuring [h]all others being obedient to our laws, and

[n] *add* generally remembered

[o] *om.* in [1]
[p-p] our counsels hath been in our government for the government and ruling of our subjects of all estates and that the same
[q-q] *omit*
[r] *add* that being
[s-s] the same
[t] *add* and seditious
[u] *add* clearly
[v-v] led and cast into, which
[w] drawn
[x] *add* allegiance and natural
[y] and

[z-z] to the end

[a] *add* likewise

[b] kinds

[c] *add* evil

[d-d] reformation of
[e-e] as be or shall be
[f] *add* and obstinately
[g] *add* speedily and earnestly against
[h-h] *omit*

i] *add* to all others being obedient to us and our laws
j   *add* freely
k   *add* mildness
l   *add* be made to
m *om.* secret
n   for
o   in
p   *add* their
q   *add* remitting that to the supreme and singular authority of Almighty God, who is the only searcher of hearts[17]
r–r all our good loving and obedient subjects
s–s into any
t–t gracious determination and grant by the
u   *add* any
v   *add* to be stirred up

w *add* against

x of
y–y *omit*[19]
z *add* notably

a–a *omit*

b *add* contempt of our Crown, breach of the public peace,
c *add* speedily
d separate

that[h] in the word of a Prince, and the presence of God[i], that they shall[j] certainly and quietly have and enjoy the fruits of our former accustomed favour[k] lenity and grace in all causes[16] requisite, without any molestation to[l] them by any person by way of examination or inquisition of their secret[m] opinions in[n] their consciences, for[o] matters of[p] faith[q]. And further we do admonish [r]all such obedient subjects to beware[r] that they be not brought [s]in[s] doubt of this our [t]grant by any[t] imagination of[u] lewd and seditious reports and tales[v] at any time hereafter, when[18] they shall behold or hear report of the execution of justice against traitors and seditious persons or[w] manifest contemners and offenders against[x] our laws; whereunto we have lately [y]to our grief[y], been so[z] provoked in sundry places by open traitorous acts and attempts, as without the notable [a]diminution of our honour[a], peril of our state[b], and manifest danger of our good subjects, we can not forbear but[c] repress such traitorous attempts, and divide[d] them according to their deserts from the rest of the sound body of our Realm, by order of justice.

[16] Burghley draft: "in all our causes".

[17] See the similar provision in the Queen's order in the Star Chamber, *post*, p. 55.

[18] Burghley draft: "whensoever".

[19] The omission of this phrase by Elizabeth is very characteristic. She would not express regret for the executions which had taken place, cruel and excessive though others felt them to be.

Finally considering the[e] multitude of our good[f] people[g] are unlearned, and thereby not able by reading hereof to conceive [h]our mind[h] and favourable disposition towards the good and obedient, nor our determination [i]and displeasure[i] by way of justice against the obstinate and disobedient, We will that, beside the ordinary[j] publication hereof[k] in all the accustomed places of our Realm, all curates in their parish churches shall at sundry[l] times as the Bishops and ordinaries shall [m]appoint[m], read this our admonition to their parishioners[n].

e *add* greater
f *om.* good
g *add* of the lowest sort

h–h and keep in mind this our admonition

i–i *omit*

j *add* manner of
k *add* to be made

l such
m–m think meet and right
n *add* in such sort as none may hereafter pretend any ignorance hereof[20]

[20] The simple folk had only offended by following those who were their natural leaders. This is to be made impossible for the future.

APPENDIX

No. I

Brief from Pius V to the Rebel Earls

[First printed in *Apostolicarum Pii Quinti Pont. Max. Epistolarum Libri Quinque. Nunc primum in lucem editi opera et cura* Francisci Goubau. Antverpiae, ex officina Plantiniana Balthasaris Moreti, M.DC.XL.; lib. IV, ep. X, pp. 290 f. It was reprinted, with a translation, in the seventeenth-century tract *A Brief Historical Account of the Behaviour of the Jesuites ... for the First Twenty-five Years of Queen Elizabeth's Reign*, which was included in Bishop Gibson's *Preservative from Popery* (vol. xvii, p. 27 f., ed. Cumming); and subsequently, with a revised translation, by Joseph Mendham in his *Life and Pontificate of Saint Pius the Fifth*, London, 1832 (the text at p. 254, the translation at p. 128). It is here reproduced from the latter work.

The genuineness of the Brief is indisputable. Francis Goubau was entirely loyal to the Papacy, and had gathered the collection of Briefs of Pope Pius V, which he afterwards published, whilst he was at Rome, serving the legate of the King of Spain to the Holy See as his secretary. And even if the external evidence were more doubtful, internal evidence would make it clear that the letter is what it professes to be.]

Dilectis Filiis, Thamae Comiti Northumbriae, et

"To our beloved sons, Thomas, Earl of North-

Carolo Comiti Weste-
merlandiae in Anglia.

Dilecti Filii, nobiles
viri, salutem et Aposto-
licam benedictionem. Ex
litteris v e s t r i s VIII.
Novembris die ad nos
datis, quibus XVI. Feb-
ruarii ad nos allatis subito
rescripsimus,[1] istius floren-
tissimi Regni miserias et
calamitates, ne a n t e a
quidem nobis incognitas,
certius subtiliusque cog-
noscentes, eo animi dolore
affecti sumus, quem et
eorum malorum quae in
vobis patimur indignitas,
et paternus noster erga vos
caeterosque Catholicos in
isto Regno viros animus
nobis afferre debuit. Nam
praeter illud commune
Pastoralis charitatis offi-
cium, quo in omnium
Christi fidelium, singular-
umque Provinciarum in
quibus nomen colitur
Christianum, salute vel
calamitate laetari aut

umberland, and Charles,
Earl of Westmorland, in
England:

"Beloved Sons, noble-
men, health and apostolic
benediction. — By your
letter of the 8th of November to us, to which, being
delivered on the 16th of
February, we returned a
s p e e d y answer, being
made more certainly and
intimately acquainted
with the miseries and
calamities, hitherto un-
known, of that highly
flourishing country, we
were affected with that
grief of mind, which both
the indignity of the evils
which we share with you,
and the paternal affection
which we bear towards
you and the other Catho-
lics of that kingdom,
ought to produce. For,
besides that common duty
of pastoral charity with
which we ought to rejoice
in the welfare, and be
grieved at the calamity, of

[1] The letter of the Earls, doubtless sent from Topcliffe just before
the meeting alluded to above (p. 14), must have been greatly delayed
on the way if it only reached its destination on 16 February. The
explanation is doubtless to be found in the fact that the English ports
were carefully guarded.

dolere debemus; praecipua quadam amoris benevolentiaeque praerogativa erga istud Regnum afficimur, quod beatissimi Gregorii Romani Pontificis praedecessoris nostri post Deum Omnipotentem opera atque industria a cultu lignorum ac lapidum aliquando ad Christianam Fidem conversum, moribus doctrinaque Catholica per idoneos viros isthuc ab eo missos institutum esse meminimus; quodque egregiam fidem devotionisque sinceritatem Apostolicae Sedi praestare consueverat. Itaque quantopere vestris Regnique istius malis his, quae eisdem litteris non minus vere quam miserabiliter deploravistis, doleamus ac conturbemur, non facile verbis consequi possemus. Dolemus tot tantaque nefariarum haeresium venena, tamque mortifera Reipublicae Christianae vulnera, in nostri Pontificatus tempora potissimum incidisse: conturbamur,

all the faithful of Christ, and of every province in which the Christian name is professed, we are affected with a certain eminent prerogative of love and benevolence towards that kingdom, both because we remember it was formerly, by the labour and industry of our own predecessor, the most blessed Gregory, bishop of Rome, after the Omnipotent God, converted from the worship of wood and stones to the Christian faith, and by fit men sent thither by him instructed in manners, and in the Catholic doctrine; and because it was used to exhibit to the apostolic See an excellent faith and sincerity of devotion. It cannot, therefore, be easily expressed in words, how much we are distressed and disturbed by the evils of yourselves, and of that kingdom which, not less truly than pathetically, you deplore in your letter. We lament that so many

quia de vestro caeterorumque Catholicorum periculo soliciti esse cogimur. Sed tamen cum ejus orationis efficaciam recordamur. qui pro B. Petro, ne ejus deficeret fides, rogavit, quique, Ecclesiam suam in tribulatione dilatans, eo admirabilius occulti sui consilii providentia gubernat, quo magis eam perturbationum fluctibus cernit agitari; non desperamus, quin quod aliis temporibus factum esse accepimus, idem nostris quoque, adjuvante Domino, fieri possit: ut quae haereticorum invalescente persecutione saepe visa fuerit conculcari, haec eadem, Domino cum ea signum in bonum faciente, in antiquae felicitatis statum redeat; et in eo incrementum accipiat, in quo visa sit detrimentum pertulisse. Ecce enim nunc, qui ex veteribus nova, et ex novis vetera facit, Dominus noster JESUS CHRISTUS, per vos charissimos viros non

and so great poisons of the most infamous heresies and such deadly wounds inflicted on the Christian republic should more especially happen in the time of our pontificate: we are troubled, because we are compelled to be solicitous about your and other Catholics' danger. Yet, when we remember the efficacy of *His* prayer, who entreated for the blessed Peter, that his faith might not fall [*sic*], and who, by extending his church under tribulation, governs it the more admirably by the providence of his secret counsel, as he beholds it agitated by the waves of perturbation; we do not despair that the same will be done in our times, with God's assistance, as we learn was done in other times; that the very church which often seemed by the prevailing persecution of heretics to be trodden under foot, should, the Lord giving a sign for that purpose for good, return to her an-

minus generis nobilitate quam Catholicae pietatis studio insignes, veterem Ecclesiae Romanae Regnique istius conjunctionem renovare et confirmare fortasse constituit; ac propterea mentem istam vestrae Fidei Catholicae zelo dignissimam vobis injecit, ut vos, Regnumque istud ex turpissima muliebris libidinis servitute ereptum, ad pristinam hujus sanctae Romanae Sedis obedientiam revocare tentaretis. Quem quidem pium ac religiosum animi vestri conatum, sicut aequum est, debitis in Domino laudibus commendantes, et ea, quam petitis, benedictione nostra prosequentes, Nobilitates vestras ad nostram hujusque sacrosanctae Sedis, cujus se auctoritati subjiciunt, potestatem tutelamque confugientes, ea qua decet benignitate recipimus atque excipimus: hortantes vos in Domino, et quo majore possumus animi nostri studio rogantes, ut in hac

tient state of felicity, and acquire increase by the very means by which she seemed to sustain detriment. For behold now, He, who of old makes new, and of new old, our Lord JESUS CHRIST, by you, who are most dear to us, no less by nobility of birth than by the prosecution of Catholic piety, has perhaps determined to restore and confirm the antient union of the Roman church and the kingdom; and has therefore inspired you with a mind so worthy of the zeal of your Christian faith as to urge you to the attempt, to deliver yourselves and that kingdom from the basest servitude of a woman's lust, and to recover them to the primitive obedience of this holy Roman See: which pious and religious endeavour of your minds we commend with due praises in the Lord; and bestowing upon it that benediction of ours which you seek, with the benignity which becomes us, we

tam egregia voluntate laudabilique instituto vestro constanter persevereetis: pro comperto habentes, Omnipotentem Deum, cujus perfecta sunt opera, quique vos ad bene de Religione Catholica in isto Regno merendum excitavit, vobis auxilio, suo affuturum. Quod si etiam in asserenda Catholica Fide, hujusque sanctae Sedis auctoritate, mors esset vobis oppetenda, profundendusque sanguis, multo praestat pro Dei confessione gloriosae mortis compendio ad aeternam vitam convolare, quam turpiter et ignominiose viventes impotentis foeminae cupiditati cum animae vestrae detrimento servire. Nolite enim putare, dilecti Filii in CHRISTO, male cum illis vel Episcopis vel Principibus istius Regni Catholicis, quos nominatis, actum esse: qui quoniam a Fidei Catholicae confessione deficere noluerunt, aut in carceres conjecti aut aliis suppliciis

receive your honourable persons fleeing to the power and protection of us and of this Holy See, to whose authority they subject themselves; exhorting you in the Lord, and with the greatest possible earnestness of our mind entreating you, to persevere constantly in this your so exceedingly good will and laudable purpose; being assured, that the Omnipotent God, whose works are perfect, and who has excited you to deserve well of the Catholic faith in that kingdom, will be present to your assistance. But if, in asserting the Catholic faith and the authority of this Holy See, you should hazard death and spill your blood, far better is it, for the confession of God, to fly by a compendious and glorious death, to eternal life, than, living basely and ignominiously, to serve the will of an impotent woman, with the injury of your souls. For think not, beloved

immerentes affecti sunt: horum enim constantiam, etiam nunc recenti, ut arbitramur, beati Thomae Archiepiscopi Cantuarensis[2] exemplo confirmatam, nemo satis pro dignitate laudare potest. Hanc eandem vos quoque imitati, forti constantique animo estote, nec ullorum periculorum denuntiatione aut minis ab incepto desistite: potens est enim Deus, in quo spem vestram repositam habere debetis, qui Pharaonis currum et exercitum ejus projecit in mare, adversariorum suorum vires potentiamque frangere, sic ut per vos pristina Religio et antiqua dignitas isti Regno restituatur. Quod quidem ut fiat, nos non solum his quae postulatis apud eos quos vultis Christianos Principes fungendis officiis adjuvabimus, sed etiam ea

sons in Christ, that those Catholic b i s h o p s or princes of that kingdom whom you name, are ill dealt with; who, because they would not forsake the profession of the Catholic faith, are either imprisoned, or are undeservedly visited with other punishments; for the constancy of these men, which is even now confirmed by a recent example, as we think, of the blessed Thomas, archbishop of Canterbury, no man can commend according to its worth. Imitating yourselves this same constancy, be of a courageous and constant mind, and desist not from the enterprize for any denunciation of danger or threatenings: for God, in whom you ought to repose your trust, who plunged the chariot and army in Pharoah in the sea, is able to break the

---

[2] I.e., Thomas Becket.

[3] He had already sent one supply of money: see *ante*, p. 13, note 1.

[4] Ridolfi, a Florentine banker in London, who acted as the Pope's confidential agent without incurring the least suspicion. The following year he left London, and soon became famous, or infamous, in connexion with the so-called Ridolfi Plot.

pecuniae summa in praesentia conferenda, quam pro nostris viribus petentibus vobis suppeditare poterimus[3]; quemadmodum a d i l e c t o Filio Roberto Rodulfo[4] clarius et copiosius intelligetis; daturi quoque operam, ut aliquanto etiam majorem, quam quantum virium nostrarum imbecillitas ferre potest, conferamus, piumque conatum vestrum omnibus, quibus cum Domino poterimus rebus facultatibusque nostris, prompto atque alacri a n i m o adjuvemus. — Datum Romae apud sanctum Petrum sub annulo Piscatoris, die xx. Februarii, M.D.LXX., Pontificatus nostri anno quinto.

strength and power of his enemies, so that by you the pristine religion and its antient dignity may be restored to that kingdom: which, that it may be effected, we will not only assist by performing the offices which you desire with Christian princes, but by immediately granting the sum of money which, according to our power, and, agreeably to your request, we are able to supply as you will understand more clearly and fully by our beloved son Robert Rodulfus; using our endeavour to contribute hereafter a greater sum than the imbecility of our means can bear, and, with a prompt and cheerful mind, to assist your pious endeavour with all our property and power, as we are able in the Lord.

Given at Rome, at St Peter's, under the seal of the Fisherman, the xxth day of February, M.D.LXX., in the fifth year of our pontificate."

No. II

Elizabeth's Declaration in the Star Chamber

(Given by Strype, *Annals of the Reformation*, vol. 1, part ii, p. 371, ed. Oxford, 1824. I have been unable to find the original. "None of the Orders or Decrees of this Court are known to exist. In the Report of a Committee of the House of Lords made in 1719, it is stated that 'the last notice of them that could be got was that they were in a house in St Bartholomew's Close, London,' and it is to be feared that they have been destroyed."—Scargill-Bird, *Guide to the Public Records*, p. 190.)

"Where as certain rumours are carried and spread abroad among sundry her Majesty's subjects, that her Majesty hath caused, or will hereafter cause, inquisition and examination to be had of men's consciences in matters of religion; her Majesty would have it known, that such reports are utterly unture, and grounded either of malice, or of some fear more than there is cause. For although certain persons have been lately convented before her Majesty's council upon just causes, and that some of them have been treated withal upon some matter of religion; yet the cause thereof hath grown merely of themselves; in that they have first manifestly broken the laws established for religion, in not coming at all to the church, to common prayer, and divine service, as of late time before they were accustomed, and had used by the space of nine or ten whole years together: so as if thereby they had not given

manifest occasion by their open and wilful contempt of breaking of her Majesty's laws, they had not been any thing molested, or dealt withal.

"Wherefore her Majesty would have all her loving subjects to understand that, as long as they shall openly continue in the observation of her laws, and shall not wilfully and manifestly break them by their open actions, her Majesty's meaning is, not to have any of them molested by any inquisition or examination of their consciences in causes of religion; but will accept and entreat them as her good and obedient subjects. And if any shall otherwise by their open deeds and facts declare themselves wilfully disobedient to break her laws; then she cannot but use them according to their deserts, and will not forbear to inquire of their demeanours, and of what mind and disposition they are, as by her laws her Majesty shall find it necessary.

"Of all which, her Majesty would have her subjects in all parts of her realm discreetly warned and admonished, not to be abused by such untrue reports, to bring them any wise to doubt of her Majesty's honourable intention towards them: Who meaneth not to enter into the inquisition of any men's consciences, as long as they shall observe her laws in their open deeds: being also very loath to be provoked by the overmuch boldness and wilfulness of her subjects to alter her natural clemency into a princely severity."